The Oregon Trail

James P. Burger

The Rosen Publishing Group's

PowerKids Press™

New York

For Kate Wittenberg, pioneer of a frontier without trails

Published in 2002 by The Rosen Publishing Group, Inc.
29 East 21st Street, New York, NY 10010

First Edition

Book Design: Emily Muschinske
Project Editor: Kathy Campbell

Photo Credits: pp. 5 (background), 13, 17 (Chimney Rock), 17 (Castle Rock), 17 (Independence Rock), 22 © James L. Amos/National Geographic; pp. 5 (inset), 6 (man on horse), 18 (top) © The Granger Collection, New York; pp. 6 (map), 13 (tonic), 20 © Hulton Getty/Archive Photos; pp. 9 (accordion), 9 (watch), 9 (tin), 9 (wagon parts), 17 (wagon train), 21 (wheel) © James L. Amos/CORBIS; p. 10 (top) © David David Gallery, Philadelphia/SuperStock; p. 10 (bottom) © The Huntington Library; pp. 13 (background), 18 (bottom) © The Huntington Library, Art Collections, and Botanical Gardens, San Marino, California/SuperStock; p. 14 (top), 20 © Lowell Georgia/CORBIS; p. 14 (bottom) © SuperStock.

Burger, James P.
The Oregon Trail / James P. Burger— 1st ed.
  p. cm. — (The library of the westward expansion)
Includes index.
  ISBN 0-8239-5850-7
1. Oregon National Historic Trail—Juvenile literature. 2. Overland journeys to the Pacific—Juvenile literature. 3. Frontier and pioneer life—West (U.S.)—Juvenile literature. 4. Frontier and pioneer life—Oregon—Juvenile literature. [1. Oregon National Historic Trail. 2. Overland journeys to the Pacific. 3. Frontier and pioneer life—West (U.S.)] I. Title.
  F597 .B9 2002
  978'.02–dc21
                                                                                    00–012479

Manufactured in the United States of America

Contents

Moving to Oregon

"Wagons ho!" With these words called out, hundreds of thousands of men, women, and children headed west on the Oregon Trail during the mid-1800s. They packed their covered wagons in the East and joined others for the dangerous, exciting voyage to the Oregon **Territory**. The East was growing crowded. People kept moving west to settle and plant their crops. Western Oregon seemed like a perfect place to farm. It had large amounts of unsettled land with fertile soil. Traveling along the Oregon Trail to get there, though, was very hard. **Emigrants** followed the trail for nearly six months, through strange territories, to their new homes in what is now the northwestern United States. The U.S. government planned to expand the country from the Atlantic Ocean to the Pacific Ocean. This idea was called **Manifest Destiny**.

Right: *The wagon-wheel ruts along the Oregon Trail still can be seen today near Burnt Ranch, Wyoming.* Inset: *This picture, from 1871, is called* Pilgrims of the Plains. *It shows members of a wagon train camping at night.*

Top: *This map shows the Oregon Trail's route, which wound along rivers, through streams, up mountains, and across deserts.* Left: *Fur trappers traveling alone were called mountain men. They used parts of the trail before emigrants took the route to the West.*

Making the Trail

In May 1843, farmer Jesse Applegate led nearly 1,000 people on the Oregon Trail, but long before that, Native Americans had settled the West. Native Americans knew the best routes through their part of the countryside and wore short footpaths across the land by traveling them often. By the early 1800s, the Western Territories were beginning to **attract** white settlers, mostly fur trappers. They hoped to make a living by hunting animals and selling furs. The trail seemed too difficult for most people to follow, but in 1836, Marcus Whitman arrived in Oregon with his wife and two **missionaries**. He built a mission and proved to people back East that they also could make the trip.

DID YOU KNOW?

Many mountain men hunted for furs, but others lived out West simply to have adventures. These men connected many rugged Native American footpaths into the 2,000-mile-long (3,219-km-long) Oregon Trail.

What to Take?

Each spring during the mid-1800s, cities like Independence, Missouri, and Council Bluffs, Iowa, bustled with eager emigrants preparing for the Oregon Trail. They spent months planning and hoped to cross the mountains into Oregon before winter. Some people tried to take their entire households with them, jamming iron stoves, rugs, and furniture into their small covered wagons. Most emigrants were wiser, though. They had heard stories about how difficult the trail could be. Too many useless items would slow them down. These people took only **necessities**, such as dried food and clothing. They also carried certain remedies for treating illness or disease, such as special tonics or powders. Travelers often came down with **scurvy**, a disease that is caused by a lack of **vitamin C**. They could treat this disease by eating fruits, vegetables, and vinegar.

Above: *Parts of covered wagons still can be seen in Wyoming near the Oregon Trail.*

Left: *An accordion, a watch, and a tobacco tin were among the items used by travelers on the Oregon Trail.*

Right: *A family takes shelter under the canvas top of their prairie schooner. People who took needless items, like cabinets and desks, often were sorry that they had. To lighten their loads, they had to leave the items scattered along the trail.*

Bottom: *Wagon trains created a lot of dust and noise on the trail. Every wagon had a certain position within the train. To make the positions fair, so that one wagon did not lead always while the others ate its dust, a different wagon led each day.*

Covered Wagons

Emigrants needed a small, sturdy wagon to make the trip along the Oregon Trail. Most emigrants chose to **modify** their farm wagons. The wheels and the axles, on which the wheels turned, were made to be strong and straight. The wooden wagon body was sealed with tar to protect supplies against the weather. A heavy, waterproof cloth, pulled tight over an upside-down U-shaped frame, covered the body. During storms, this cover could protect the travelers. The wagons were small and tightly packed. Many emigrants rode horses, but most walked alongside the wagons during pleasant weather. Only small children or sick people rode up front in the wagon.

DID YOU KNOW?

A common name for the covered wagons was prairie schooners. They often looked like schooners, a type of sailboat, sailing across the windy, grass prairies of places like today's Kansas and Nebraska. Two or four horses or oxen usually pulled the prairie schooners.

Unexpected Dangers

Nearly every man crossing the Oregon Trail carried a gun. They expected to **encounter** fierce Native American warriors, like those in the wild stories that they had heard in the East. The wagon trains did not get far before meeting Native Americans who were friendly and who wanted to trade. People wrote home about the kind Native Americans, who sometimes guided wagon trains along parts of the trail. The emigrants told of their own true experiences with them.

There were unexpected dangers along the way, though. Guns misfired, people fell from wagons, children were crushed by wagon wheels, and the emigrants carried a disease called cholera. The trail became lined with gravestones because of cholera. Some Native Americans got the disease from emigrants. These Native Americans took it back to their camps. Many of the others at these camps died from cholera, too.

Left: *Gravestones lined the Oregon Trail, many because of cholera.*

Right: *An ad for ginger tonic shows a traveler reviving an emigrant with a dose of the beverage. The ad claims that the tonic is a cure for cholera and other illnesses.*

DR. C. Y. GIRARD'S
GINGER BRANDY.

"A CERTAIN CURE" for Cholera Colic Cramps Dysentery, Chills & Fever, is a delightful & healthy beverage.

FOR SALE HERE.

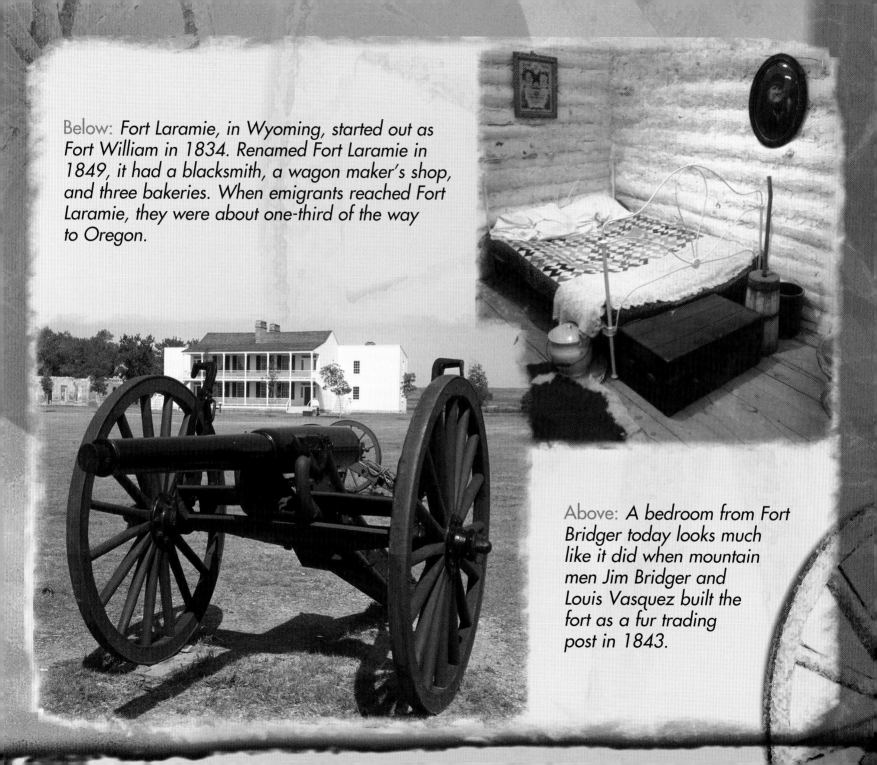

Below: Fort Laramie, in Wyoming, started out as Fort William in 1834. Renamed Fort Laramie in 1849, it had a blacksmith, a wagon maker's shop, and three bakeries. When emigrants reached Fort Laramie, they were about one-third of the way to Oregon.

Above: A bedroom from Fort Bridger today looks much like it did when mountain men Jim Bridger and Louis Vasquez built the fort as a fur trading post in 1843.

Forts

Five forts built by fur trappers and the U.S. Army aided the emigrants during their trip to Oregon. Some offered more services than others. Fort Kearny, along the Platte River in Nebraska, was the first fort the emigrants reached after leaving Independence or St. Joseph, Missouri. People used it mostly as a post office. **Mountain men** Jim Bridger and Louis Vasquez built Fort Bridger in Wyoming in 1843. The fort had a store, a fur trading post, and a place for people to rest. Forts provided more than just supplies or a place to rest, though. They also helped the emigrants keep track of the distance they had traveled. The forts' soldiers often protected the travelers from the dangers on the Oregon Trail.

DID YOU KNOW?

Two forts in Idaho became major stops on the route. Fort Hall was a well-stocked trading post, but Fort Boise, the last fort before Oregon, may have been the most pleasing sight. At Fort Boise, emigrants could restock their supplies that, by that time, had run dangerously low in the small wagons.

Sights to See

The Western Territories looked very different from the lands back East, and that made the trip exciting. At night, when there was extra time before going to bed, people told stories or sang around campfires. The emigrants put all the covered wagons in a circle at night to protect their camp. Then they felt safe in the **vast** Western Territories.

Some of the natural features of the West amazed the emigrants. In eastern Idaho, the water in the Soda Springs bubbled. The emigrants put **citric acid** and sugar in that water and drank it as though it were lemonade! There were other strange springs along the way, too. Steamboat Springs shot gas into the air and sounded like the hissing of a steamboat engine. Some hot springs, where water nearly boiled, also could be found along the trail.

Emigrants on the Oregon Trail saw many natural wonders, such as weatherworn bluffs, tall rock columns, and cliffs worn by riverbeds.

Chimney Rock, Nebraska

A wagon train on the trail

Independence Rock, Wyoming

Castle Rock, Oregon

Above: *River crossings were dangerous. Wagons might sink or people might be washed away and drowned.*

Bottom: *Ferries, like this one on the Platte River, varied in their sizes. Some small rafts were used as ferries and could hold only one wagon at a time. These small ferries often sank. The bigger, stronger ferries could carry three or four wagons at once.*

River Crossings

Most of the Oregon Trail followed the Platte, Snake, and Columbia Rivers toward the West. The wagon trains had to cross these rivers where they came to a bend. Wagons that floated made the crossing easier. Oxen dragged these wagons across the rivers, but sometimes they were too **exhausted** to swim. They got stuck in a current and drowned.

Some Native Americans and fur trappers built ferries and bridges across rivers, especially after more and more wagon trains appeared on the trail. They charged tolls for using these ferries and bridges. The tolls were expensive, but the wagon trains could cross faster and more safely by using them.

DID YOU KNOW?

Some travelers could not afford to pay the expensive tolls. Some refused to pay. They risked driving their wagons through rivers when a bridge or ferry was just within sight!

Over the Mountains

The first settlers of the West crossed the Rocky Mountains to reach their **destination**. On October 22, 1812, a Scottish fur trader named Robert Stuart discovered a 20-mile-wide (32-km-wide) gap in the Rocky Mountains. This easy route through the Rockies, near today's Casper, Wyoming, was called the South Pass. Its discovery meant that only the Blue Mountains were left for most emigrants to cross. The Blue Mountains still were dangerous, though they were not as high as the Rocky Mountains. Luckily they were the last major **obstacles** before reaching Oregon. Mountain men and Native Americans often were hired as guides to lead wagon trains through the rockiest parts of the trail. Many guides knew the area well and gave trustworthy help to the weary emigrants. Some guides only offered directions for shortcuts that led the travelers into dangerous situations.

Left: *Emigrants had a hard time crossing the steep Rockies.*

Left: Emigrants had to bring tools and spare wagon parts with them on the Oregon Trail.

Below: Travelers had to cross the Rockies before the winter or they might be stranded and starve.

The Trail's End

After crossing the Blue Mountains, the emigrants reached Oregon. Most didn't stop until they had reached the Willamette Valley in western Oregon. In Astoria,

People carved their names in soft rocks along the Oregon Trail.

emigrants could find out about the best places to live and farm. Just because they had completed their long journey did not mean the work stopped. Houses and farms needed to be built, and quickly, too. The emigrants began their voyage in the spring. Winter would meet them shortly after their arrival in Oregon. Around 300,000 people traveled to Oregon between 1843 and the late 1850s. Some wagon trains did set out after this time. The last went during the 1890s, just 20 years before the automobile was invented. Although the names scratched into Independence Rock have faded, they remind us of those who bravely helped the United States grow from sea to shining sea.

Glossary

attract (uh-TRAKT) To cause people to want to be near something.

citric acid (SIH-trik A-sihd) A sour-tasting acid in juices, like orange, lemon, and lime juice.

destination (des-teh-NAY-shun) A place to which a person is traveling or something is sent.

emigrants (EH-mih-grints) People who have left a country to settle somewhere else.

encounter (en-KOWN-ter) To meet by chance.

exhausted (eg-ZAH-sted) Very tired.

Manifest Destiny (MA-neh-fest DES-teh-nee) A phrase first used by John L. O'Sullivan in 1845 that said it was the United States's right to spread the length of the entire continent, from the Atlantic Ocean to the Pacific Ocean.

missionaries (MIH-shuh-nayr-eez) People who teach their religion to people with different beliefs.

modify (MAH-duh-fy) To change something so that it does something different from its original purpose.

mountain men (MOUN-ten MEN) Fur trappers who are at home in the wilderness.

necessities (nuh-SEH-suh-teez) Things that are needed.

obstacles (OB-stuh-kulz) Things that are in the way.

scurvy (SKER-vee) A disease caused by a lack of the vitamin C that comes from many fresh fruits like oranges and grapefruit.

territory (TEHR-uh-tohr-ee) Land that is controlled by a person or a group of people.

vast (VAST) Very large in size.

vitamin C (VY-tuh-min SEE) One of a group of substances that are needed in small amounts for the health and the normal working of the body. Vitamin C, or ascorbic acid, is found in plants, fruits, and leafy vegetables, and can be used in preventing or treating scurvy.

Index

Web Sites

Due to the changing nature of Internet links, PowerKids Press has developed an online list of Web sites related to the subject of this book. This site is updated regularly. Please use this link to access the list:
www.powerkidslinks.com/lwe/oregon/